LIFE'S LITTLE BOOK OF

faith
AND hope

LIFE'S LITTLE BOOK OF

faith
AND hope

JO PETTY

BRISTOL PARK BOOKS

Published by:

BRISTOL PARK BOOKS, INC
252 W. 38th Street, New York, NY 10018

First Bristol Park Books edition published in 2013
Bristol Park Books is a registered trademark of Bristol Park Books, Inc.

Library of Congress Control Number: 2013934057
ISBN: 978-0-88486-538-4 E-Book ISBN: 978-0-88486-539-1

Cover and text design by LaBreacht Design
Printed in the United States of America

foreword

CULLED FROM MANY different sources, these eloquent and heartfelt praises celebrate the basic Christian virtues —faith, long suffering, meekness, temperance—that have served as a cornerstone for all my devotional works.

These writings have been a constant source of inspiration and spiritual sustenance to me in my daily life, and I share them with you, my beloved readers, in the hope that they will set your hearts singing and spirits soarings.

—Jo Petty

contents

faith

None that trust in God
shall be desolate.

It is hard for those who trust in riches
to enter into the kingdom of God.

The trial of your faith
is more precious than gold.

Faith is the awareness of utter helplessness
without God.

Faith grows in the valley.

The things which are seen are temporal,
but the things which are not seen are eternal.

Ask in faith, nothing wavering.
For he that wavers is like a wave of the sea
driven with the wind and tossed.

The only ideas
that will work for you
are the ones
you put to work.

Nothing is or can be accidental
with God.

Life is eternal,
Love is immortal
and Death is only a horizon,
and a horizon is only
the limit of our sight.

Wit's end need not be the end, but the beginning.
The end of man's contriving often is
the beginning of God's arriving.

All I see teaches me to trust the Creator
for all I do not see.

A wish is a desire without any attempt
to attain its end.

Prayer without work is beggary;
work without prayer is slavery.

Don't tell me that worry doesn't do any good.
I know better.
The things I worry about don't happen.

Death is not
extinguishing the light;
it is putting out the lamp
because dawn has come.

Today is the tomorrow
you worried about yesterday.

Prayer is not a substitute for work.
It is a desperate effort to work further
and to be effective beyond the range
of one's power.

Don't be afraid to be afraid.

A skeptic is one
who won't take *know*
for an answer.

If I have faith as a grain of mustard seed,
nothing shall be impossible to me.

❧

We have access by faith into this grace wherein we stand
and rejoice in hope of the glory of God.

❧

Ask, and it shall be given to you;
seek and you shall find;
knock, and it shall be opened to you.

The past
cannot be changed;
the future is still
in your power.

The man who trusts men will make fewer mistakes
than he who distrusts them.

No man is responsible for the rightness of his faith;
but only for the uprightness of it.

The best and most beautiful things in the world
cannot be seen nor touched but are felt in the heart.

God never closes one door
without opening another.

I'll take the Bible as my guide
until something better comes along.

The body is my house—it is not I.
Triumphant in this faith I live and die.

With God, nothing shall be impossible.

Do the very best you can…
And leave the outcome to God.

Fear brings more pain than does the pain it fears.

A man is not old until regrets take the place of dreams.

Faith
is the eyesight
of the soul.

Train up a child
in the way he should go;
and when he is old,
he will not depart from it.

Of all the troubles great and small
are those that never happened at all.

If there is no way out, there is a way up.

It is only the fear of God that can deliver us
from the fear of men.

Some folks just don't seem to realize when
they're moaning about not getting prayers answered,
that NO is the answer.

Without the way, there is no going;
Without the truth, there is no knowing;
Without the life, there is no living.

It is not the greatness of my faith that moves mountains,
but my faith in the greatness of God.

The horizon
is not the boundary
of the world.

Be persuaded that, what He has promised,
He is able also to perform.

Men do not need to be instructed
how to pray in the midst of battle.

Faith does not exclude work,
but only the merit of work.

When we see the lilies spinning in distress,
Taking thought to manufacture loveliness—
When we see the birds building barns for store,
'Twill be the time for us to worry, not before.

Faith is the substance of things hoped for,
the evidence of things not seen.

Never put a question mark where God puts a period.

Faith is the victory that overcomes the world.

All unbelief is the belief of a lie.

Use your gifts faithfully,
and they shall be enlarged;
practice what you know, and
you shall attain to higher knowledge.

I fail not to apply and
God never fails to supply.

The real victory of faith is to trust God in the dark.

I pray "Thy kingdom come" and I work towards that end.

He will shield me from suffering or
He will send me unfailing strength with which to bear it.

I may pray for anything I desire.

By grace are you saved through faith;
and that not of yourselves: it is the gift of God—
not of works lest any man should boast.

The Bible is a surer and safer guide through life
than human reason.

It is impossible that anything so natural,
so necessary, and so universal as death should ever
have been designed as an evil to mankind.

Examine yourselves,
whether you be in the faith;
prove your own selves.

You have not, because you ask not.

A ship is safest in deep water.

Inexperience is what makes a young man do
what an older man says is impossible.

The sectarian thinks that he has the sea
ladled into his private pond.

Anyone can carry his burden,
however heavy, until nightfall;
anyone can do his work,
however hard, for one day.

Teach me to live that I may dread the grave
as little as my bed.

Never think that God's delays
are God's denials.

The night is not forever.

Whatever we beg
of God,
let us also
work for it.

Long suffering

People who fly
into a rage
always make
a bad landing.

There is no failure save in giving up.

⊷

A mistake at least proves somebody
stopped talking long enough to do something.

⊷

The diamond cannot be polished without friction,
nor man perfected without trials.

The secret of patience is doing
something else in the meanwhile.

The door to the room of success
swings on the hinges of opposition.

We cannot do everything at once;
but we can do something at once.

Whoever has resigned
himself to fate,
will find that fate
accepts his resignation.

Itching for what you want
doesn't do much good;
you've got to scratch for it.

We would rather be ruined by praise
than saved by criticism.

Marrying is not Marriage.

A diamond is a
piece of coal
that stuck to the job.

The Lord sometimes takes us into troubled waters
not to drown us, but to cleanse us.

I'd better not be wasting time,
for time is wasting me!

The more difficult the obstacle,
the stronger one becomes after hurdling it.

You've reached
middle age
when all you exercise
is caution.

No difficulties, no discovery,
No pains, no gains.

One thing at a time and that done well
is a very good rule as many can tell.

The secret of success is constancy to purpose.

If you can't have
the best of everything,
make the best of
everything you have.

Forget mistakes.
Organize victory out of mistakes.

Mastery in any art
comes only with long practice.

The early bird gets the firm.

It is easier to fight
for one's principles
than to live up to them.

Making excuses
doesn't change the truth.

If I could only see the road you came,
With all the jagged rocks and crooked ways,
I might more kindly think of our misstep
And only praise.

The dictionary is the only place
success comes before work.

Better limp all the way to heaven
than not get there at all.

In youth we run into difficulties;
in age difficulties run into us.

Patience is not passive; on the contrary it is active;
it is concentrated strength.

You can tell some people aren't afraid of work
by the way they fight it.

All people are born equal.
Each has a right to earn his niche by the sweat of his brow.
But some sweat more and carve larger niches.

Adversity is
the only balance
to weigh friends—
prosperity is
no just scale.

You can't slide uphill.

Make the most of the best
and least of the worst.

The way of the world is to praise dead saints
and persecute living ones.

An obstinate man
does not hold opinions—
they hold him.

Talent knows what to do;
tact knows when and how to do it.

Confront improper conduct,
not by retaliation, but by example.

Life is 10% what you make it
and 90% how you take it.

We can do anything we want
if we stick to it long enough.

Patience—in time the grass becomes milk.

Fortune does not change men.
It only unmasks them.

Be not overcome of evil,
but overcome evil with good.

Sometimes the best gain is to lose.

The only time you mustn't fail
is the time you try.

The virtue lies
in the struggle,
not in the prize.

Failing is not falling,
but in failing to rise when you fall.

Better to slip with the foot than with the tongue.

He who keeps his mouth and his tongue
keeps his soul from troubles.

The winner never quits.

There's no sense
in advertising your troubles.
There is no market for them.

When music speaks,
all other voices should cease.

Silence is not always golden—
sometimes it is just plain yellow.

Your body is for use—not abuse.

Spend less than you get.

≈

Stretching the truth
won't make it any longer.

≈

If you blame others for your failures,
do you credit others with your successes?

Those who have suffered much
are like those who know many languages;
they have learned to understand all
and to be understood by all.

Education should be as gradual as the moonrise,
perceptible not in progress but in result.

Trouble is only opportunity in work clothes.

A man can fail many times,
but he isn't a failure
until he begins to blame
somebody else.

A man's best fortune or his worst is his wife.

Before you flare up at anyone's faults,
take time to count ten—ten of your own.

The greatest calamity of all is not to have failed;
but to have failed to try.

Education isn't play and it can't be made to look like play.
It is hard, hard work, but it can be made interesting work.

Fault finders never improve the world;
they only make it seem worse than it really is.

A failure is a man who has blundered
but is not able to cash in on the experience.

Learn from the mistakes of others—
you can't live long enough to make them all yourself.

❧

Great victories come, not through ease
but by fighting valiantly and meeting hardships bravely.

❧

The grinding that would wear away to nothing a lesser stone,
merely serves to give luster to a diamond.

They also serve who only stand and wait.

Sometime, when all life's lessons have been learned,
we shall see how God's plans were right,
and how what seemed reproof was love most true.

Anytime a man takes a stand,
there'll come a time when he'll be tested
to see how firm his feet are planted.

Toil awhile, endure awhile, believe always,
and never turn back.

Fundamentally true ideas possess greater ultimate power
than physical might.

Borrowing trouble from the future
does not deplete the supply.

There are those who are ever learning
and never able to come to the knowledge of truth.

Poise is the art of raising the eyebrows
instead of the roof.

It is easier to be critical than correct.

As threshing separates the wheat from the chaff,
so does affliction purify virtue.

Recreation is not being idle;
it is easing the wearied part by change of occupation.

Let me run with patience the race that is set before me.

The rock of my strength, and my refuge, is in God.

Difficulties
strengthen the mind,
as labor does
the body.

Trying times are times for trying.

The secret of success is hard work.

It is easier to be critical than correct.

An ounce of pluck is worth a ton of luck.

Character
development
is the true aim
of education.

We first make our habits,
and then our habits make us.

No wise man ever wished to be younger.

A fool utters all his mind;
but a wise man keeps it in till afterwards.

Listening is wanting to hear.

It is by those
who have suffered
that the world
is most advanced.

It is the practice of the multitudes
to bark at eminent men as little dogs at strangers.

A just man falls seven times, and rises up again.

The aim of education is to teach us how to think,
not what to think.

The greatest and sublimest power is often simple patience.

meekness

The doorstep to the temple of wisdom
is knowledge of our own ignorance.

A peck of common sense is worth
a bushel of learning.

There's nothing wrong with being a self-made man
if you don't consider the job finished too soon.

A college education seldom hurts a man if he's willing
to learn a little something after he graduates.

No experienced man ever stigmatized
a change of opinion as inconsistency.

Lord, give me this day my daily opinion,
and forgive me the one I had yesterday.

Nonchalance is the ability to look like an owl
when you have acted like a jackass.

We see things not as they are, but as we are.

Though the Lord be high,
He has respect for the lowly.

He tried to be somebody
by trying to be like everybody,
which makes him a nobody.

Every one of us shall give account of himself to God.
Let us not therefore judge one another.

Learn from the mistakes of others—
you can't live long enough to make them all yourself.

Meekness is surrendering to God.

Children should hear
the instruction of their parents.

A meek and quiet spirit
is of great price in the sight of God.

If anyone asks you to go a mile,
go with him two.

A mighty man is not delivered by much strength.

Nothing will make us so kind and tender
to the faults of others as to thoroughly examine ourselves.

We cannot always oblige,
but we can always speak obligingly.

When success turns
a man's head,
he is facing failure.

Pride makes us esteem ourselves;
vanity desires the esteem of others.

Be sure of this:
you are dreadfully like other people.

Whosoever shall exalt himself shall be abased;
and he that shall humble himself shall be exalted.

There is no surer sign
of perfection
than a willingness
to be corrected.

The wisdom of this world
is foolishness with God.

Be not like the cock who thought the sun rose
to hear him crow.

The man who leaves home to set the world on fire
often comes back for more matches.

When you think you stand,
take heed lest you fall.

Meekness is not weakness.

A child can ask many questions
the wisest man cannot answer.

When young, consider that one day
you will be old and when old,
remember you were once young.

To know how to grow old
is the master work of wisdom,
and one of the most difficult
chapters in the great art of living.

The greatest undeveloped territory in the world
lies under your hat.

If we resist our passions,
it is more through their weakness than our strength.

Never forget that you are a part of the people
who can be fooled some of the time.

There is nothing permanent but change.

Past experience should be a guide post, not a hitching post.

Life is like a ladder.
Every step we take is either up or down.

A philosopher is someone who always knows
what to do until it happens to him.

Quite often when a man thinks
his mind is getting broader,
it is only his conscience stretching.

Receive with meekness the engrafted Word
which is able to save your soul.

Before honor
is humility.

I am only one, but I am one.
I cannot do everything, but I can do something.

A man's life does not consist in the abundance
of things which he possesses.

I am the clay, and God is the potter:
and I am the work of His Hand!

Many might have attained wisdom had they not thought
that they had already attained it.

Every man I meet is in some way my superior;
and in that I can learn from him.

It makes a man sort of humble to have been
a kid when everything was the kid's fault
and a parent at a time when everything
is the parent's fault.

Learn to be content
in whatsoever
state you are.

The purpose of education is to provide everyone with
the opportunity to learn how best he may serve the world.

A learned man always has wealth within himself.

Everyone is ignorant—only on different subjects.

They that know God will be humble;
they that know themselves cannot be proud.

An open mind leaves a chance
for someone to drop
a worthwhile thought in it.

May I remember that mankind got along
very well before my birth and in all probability
will get along very well after my death.

To accept good advice is but to increase one's own ability.

Knowledge makes men humble,
and true genius is ever modest.

We may be taught
by every person we meet.

If you have knowledge
let others light their candles by it.

Understanding is a wellspring of life
unto him who has it.

Wealth gotten by vanity shall be diminished;
but he that gathers by labor shall increase.

An admission of error is a sign of strength
rather than a confession of weakness.

≈

God resists the proud,
but gives grace to the humble.

≈

The more you know,
the more you know you don't know.

The ways of man are before
the eyes of the Lord,
and he ponders all his goings.

The test of good manners is being able
to put up pleasantly with bad ones.

The greatest truths are the simplest
and so are the greatest men.

Do you care for the poor at your door?

I have wept in the night
for the shortness of sight
that to somebody's need made me blind.
But I never have yet
felt a twinge of regret
for being a little too kind.

In honor prefer one another.

True politeness is perfect ease and freedom;
it simply consists in treating others
as you love to be treated yourself.

Few things are more bitter than to feel bitter.

If you are not for yourself, who will be for you?

Listening is a way of loving.

Teach thy tongue to say,
"I do not know."

temperance

Frugality is good if liberality be joined by it.

The driver is safer when the roads are dry;
the roads are safer when the driver is dry.

People who fly into a rage
always make a bad landing.

The archer who overshoots
his mark does no better
than he who falls short of it.

It is better to keep your mouth shut and be thought a fool
than it is to open it and prove it.

Habit is a cable; we weave a thread of it everyday,
and at last we cannot break it.

In times of crisis we must avoid both ignorant change
and ignorant opposition to change.

We always weaken
what we exaggerate.

If your outgo exceeds your income,
then your upkeep will be your downfall.

Gossip is the art of saying nothing
in a way that leaves nothing unsaid.

Do you spend more than you make
on things you don't need
to impress people you don't like?

No man is free
who cannot
command himself.

Money may not go as far as it used to,
but we have just as much trouble getting it back.

Sooner throw a pearl at hazard
than an idle or useless word;
and do not say a little in many words,
but a great deal in a few.

Habit is either the best of servants
or the worst of masters.

Silence is one of the great arts
of conversation.

Being overly careful about tiny details of one virtue
can't make up for complete neglect of another duty.

≈

No gain is so certain as that which proceeds
from the economical use of what you already have.

≈

Thrift is a wonderful thing—
and who doesn't wish his ancestors had practiced it more?

I have often regretted
my speech,
seldom my silence.

I shall never be deceived more by another
than by myself.

The chains of habit are generally too small to be felt
until they are too strong to be broken.

Seconds count, especially when dieting.

Silence is a talent as greatly
to be cherished as that other asset,
the gift of speech.

Often the difference between a successful marriage
and a mediocre one consists of leaving
about three or four things a day unsaid.

The longer you keep
your temper the more
it will improve.

In any controversy the instant we feel anger
we have already ceased striving for truth,
and have begun striving for ourselves.

Dignity is the capacity to hold back
on the tongue what never should have been
in the mind in the first place.

Even moderation ought not to be practiced to excess.

The real problem of your leisure
is how to keep other people from using it.

Besides the noble art of getting things done,
there is the noble art of leaving things undone.
The wisdom of life consists
in the elimination of nonessentials.

Too many people quit looking for work
when they find a job.

Meekness, temperance:
against such there is no law.

I cannot conquer fate and necessity, but I can yield to them
in such a manner as to be greater than if I could.

Death and life are in the power of the tongue.

I may not be able to change my circumstances,
but I can change my attitude toward them.

He that retrains his lips is wise.

When a man has not a good reason
for doing a thing, he has one good reason
for letting it alone.

Prosperity's right hand is industry,
and her left hand is frugality.

The safest way to double your money
is to fold it over once and put it in your pocket.

Waste of time is the most
extravagant and costly
of all expenses.

A penny saved is as good as a penny earned.

∽

Leisure for men of business and business for men
of leisure would cure many complaints.

∽

Gold has been the ruin of many.

Wealth is a means to an end
and not the end itself.

Some live without working
and others work without living.

Speech is the index of the mind.

Think little
of what others
think of you.

Hard work is an accumulation
of easy things you didn't do
when you should have.

"The longest way 'round is the shortest way home."
"Make haste slowly." "Haste makes waste."
These are all homely proverbs with the same meaning;
namely, careful painstaking effort pays in the long run.

We always have enough time if we but use it right.

There is only a slight difference between keeping your chin up and sticking your neck out, but it's worth knowing.

Blessed is he who, having nothing to say, refrains from giving wordy evidence of the fact.

Economy is in itself
a source of great revenue.

Riches are not an end of life,
but an instrument of life.

Good luck is a lazy man's estimate
of a worker's success.

Willful waste makes
woeful want.